Alligator Woman

Alligator Woman

A Book of Poetry

ABBY ARMSTRONG

RESOURCE *Publications* • Eugene, Oregon

ALLIGATOR WOMAN
A Book of Poetry

Resource Publications
An Imprint of Wipf and Stock Publishers
199 W. 8th Ave., Suite 3
Eugene, OR 97401

www.wipfandstock.com

PAPERBACK ISBN: 979-8-3852-5463-7
HARDCOVER ISBN: 979-8-3852-5464-4
EBOOK ISBN: 979-8-3852-5465-1

08/21/25

This book is dedicated to my friends.
Thank you for keeping me tethered to what matters most.

"It is a most unreasonable fancy
that we should exist forever."
DAVID HUME

Contents

Illustrations   xi

Iridescent Souls   1

Washin' Dishes   3

To My Darling   5

Blue Dress, Purple Bikini   7

Raw   8

Pretty Lashes   9

The Moment When My Final Straw Snaps   10

The Dirty Dog   11

The Title Doesn't Matter For This One   15

I'm Glad I Forgot My Rain Jacket   16

Stranger   17

Hibernation   18

Something Witnessed At Sunset   22

The Eyes of the Creek   24

My Raven Came Home   25

Charm of the South   29

Stay   31

AVID   34

Burn Me, Baby.   35

A Perspective Beyond the Eyes   36

You have good blood.   37

It's getting late, you should get some rest.   38

He was kind.   40

Sweet Thing   42
Oak Mountain   44
Paper and Paint   46
Little Adventure   48
Careful–   49
Friendly Glances   50
Stay Here.   52
To Touch   54
Nice   55
Just Scared   56
Distance   57
Alligator Woman   58
Tall Boy with a Bible   60
The Disappointment.   63
Cracked Glass   64
Someone sent you roses!   65
Stop Pretending You Don't Wanna Touch Me   66
Persuasion of the Mind   67
The Prodigy   69
The Speech That Saved Our Marriage   70
Just Hibernating   71
To Be Content   73
The Hunt   75
Modest Girl   77
Hydra   79
Return Label & Receipt   81
Talk   82
Why don't you whine a little louder?   83
Menelaus Blue Morphos   85
Circle Driveway   86
The Coffee Shop   88
The Angel and The Deviant   89

I Am No Performer   90

Two Weeks After I Stopped Taking Birth Control   92

In the Moment   94

Ugly   96

A Chance   97

To Dad   98

Neon Angel   99

The Day I Left My Dream   100

RAGE   103

Two months after I stopped taking birth control,   105

I'm A Horrible Baker   107

Barking   109

Long Braids   111

Eye Contact   113

See Me Ruin   114

My Nature   115

I Am A Fearful Creature   116

Smiling at a Stranger   117

ILLUSTRATIONS

Washin' Dishes—Vada Snuggs   4

The Dirty Dog—Vada Snuggs   13

My Raven Came Home—Vada Snuggs   26

Charm of the South—Vada Snuggs   30

Paper and Paint—Cecily Downey   47

Alligator Woman—Vada Snuggs   59

Tall Boy with a Bible—Cecily Downey   61

The Hunt—Cecily Downey   76

Modest Girl—Cecily Downey   78

I'm A Horrible Baker—Vada Snuggs   108

Barking—Vada Snuggs   110

Long Braids—Cecily Downey   112

Smiling at a Stranger—Cecily Downey   119

IRIDESCENT SOULS

Colors trickle over your skin like water,
each shade reflected in a kaleidoscope
of vibrant buoyancy. You're constantly moving
and always watching. You like to watch
the birds, try to dissect their tweedy conversations.
Analyzing tilted feathered heads—you make up half
of the chirps meaning. Just for the hell of it. Just for fun.

Colors cling to your smile like honey,
a sweet taste oozing into your laughter
and charm. The first time you turned
your full attention to me, I felt as if I was staring
at a painting. But not a hundred-year-old canvas
hung in a museum—you were being painted live
in front of me. Not a single color had time to dry
because you'll paint as long as your blood moves.

Colors kiss the curves of your body, ever-changing
bruises scattered around by your adventurous,
uninhibited nature. As we grew closer, I found myself
trying to define you, put you in a box so you were easier
for me to comprehend. I soon realized my efforts were useless.
My best guess was this: human. You're good at not hurting
people because you've done it before and regretted it. You're
not afraid to change and I am terrified to.

You hold peace in one hand and chaos in the other. Both are equal and important. It wasn't until you put your hands together that I realized:

They are one in the same. Just like the colors—every shade no more than a trick of the light, a shift in movement, as they all become one in the end. I've spent hours upon hours staring at one shade of my life, one problem I just can't solve. If only I had realized sooner—all I had to do was move. Shift, shuffle, step, just something to make the colors change. As I leaned into the iridescence, I acquired the acceptance in life that makes you so brave.

So that's why I'm walking away. I have to leave if I want to grow. I have no doubt
you will encourage my departure—with bittersweet, colorful tears in your eyes.
I hope one day, those colors will pull us together once more—like two iridescent souls.

WASHIN' DISHES

You're telling me about your day,
the faucet's runnin' too hot on my
hands but I don't notice cus' you're
eyes are glittering in the sunlight—
like diamonds twinkling
in a language only shared with stars.
I'm washing the dishes and thinking
about how many lifetimes it would
take me to understand the absolute
determination with which you love
every living creature you can get
your hands on. Sometimes my gut
becomes a shadow because I am
forced to watch the waves of
empathy drown out everything
around you. I could shout your name
and you wouldn't hear an echo—
to love is to lose and to lose is to touch,
and you love what you know you're
going to lose because you figured out
the best lovers are the ones you can't keep.
I know what it's like to drown in the waters
of someone else's pain. I know how bad
the sting hits once you realize you care more
than they do. You take every punch twice
and oh, those bruises *burn* once you find out
the other person never took a hit.

I guess that's why it's easy for me to hold you.
We know each other's pain better than anyone else.
You're telling me about your day,
the faucet's turned cold enough
to numb my hands but I don't move cus'
I've just realized you're about to leave me.

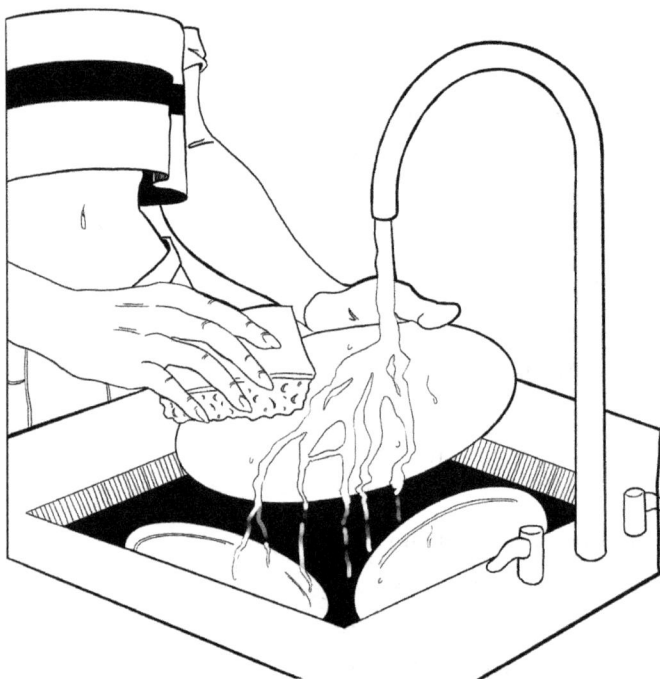

TO MY DARLING

You know, I realized the other day
while staring out our bedroom window—
I never buried you.

We used to play cards every Thursday afternoon
right by this window. I'd stare at the setting sun,
then at you, and I would always be dazzled
by how your beauty glowed in the trickling
light of dusk. You truly shined in those moments—
in the small, fragmented pieces of my memory.
I remember the day your family moved into
the neighborhood. You were clinging to your
father's knee like a frail old woman clinging
tight onto her cane. You were so afraid that if
you let go, your whole life would be over.
My mother and I brought chocolate chip cookies
to your house. When your father opened the door,
your form still clinging onto him in the dark
of the doorway, I felt as if I were staring at a statue.
You hardly moved and I kept anxiously waiting
for you to blink, to say something. It took several
weeks before you had the courage to ask if I wanted
to come over and play dress up. You loved playing
pirates, imagining the limbs in the trees
were monstrous tentacles grappling at the ship,
the wind like thunderous waves testing our

balance and strength. As we grew older, the games
turned into early morning bike rides, trips to the local
drive in theater, late nights spent giggling at one another's
joy. So much time has passed now, I find myself
clinging to those moments like you clung to your father
the first day I met you. I feel as though I understand now.
I understand the fear. But I also understand the courage.
It's difficult to walk each day without your hand in mine.
But—

I never buried you because you never really died.
You're still here. I believe you always will be.
You will always exist, whether it's in the warm feeling
in my chest every time I think of you, or in the coolness
of a late-night chill clashing with the setting sun.
You will always exist, and I will always love you.

BLUE DRESS, PURPLE BIKINI

Sometimes I wonder what it'd feel like
if you put one hand on my thigh, the other
on the steering wheel.

So sweet of you, friend, to drive me home
every day after school. Do you notice the way
I stare when you smile like that?

Sometimes I wonder if you wonder
how it'd feel to push dark lips to mine,
hands slipping into places we only
dare to dream about.

Do you wish to discover what could
happen if we say yes to desire and no
to second guessing?

The blue sundress you wore to the beach,
purple bikini—salt, sand, and tension in the ocean
air. I could hardly breathe, and yet, never
felt so alive.

Tell me, how did you feel—to have me so
close, so naked, and still so far
from where you'd like to have me?

RAW

I hate the way you stare at me.
There's one reason for you—
why I don't want to be near you.
Your touch is backhanded and I
know how to stitch a wound. Do
you hear me? Can you? Is it even
possible for you to understand how
we truly differ? I'm sure you have your
own intricate qualities to share—but is
it possible? Do you want to try? Or is my
consciousness too much of an inconvenience?

I hate the way you stare at me because I
don't feel like a person. I feel like an object
of pleasure and satisfaction. You treat love
like it's an exchange economy. Where's the
integrity?

You want me naked and I want you raw.

PRETTY LASHES

It took you way too long to figure out
I wasn't an object. So, no, I don't want
you to touch me. I don't want your backhanded,
calloused caress. The way you love me
is offensive.

I'm more than just bored with your flirtations.
I feel my bones splintering into muscle
every time you tell me how pretty my skin
looks in the spring sun. "Oh, how you bloom,"
you say in mock awe.

You are not in awe of me, just my body.
Even my intellect is determined from behind
fogged lenses. How dare you act appalled
when I ask you to wipe them. "I'm clean!"
you say. I know not to believe you

because I know what you want.
Do you have any idea what you do to me
each time you ogle my tits and ass
when I'm standing *right in front of you* talking
about how fascinating the molecular structure
of water is—

I'm standing right in front of you
but you can't see beyond the lashes
you call pretty.

THE MOMENT WHEN MY FINAL STRAW SNAPS

It feels like I'm about to let
someone be cruel to me—just cus'
I think they're pretty.

It feels like I got slapped all the way
to Death County, Sheriff Reaper's
cuffs wrapped round my wrists.

It feels like a hot red warning
sign but I know I'm gonna ignore
it because I'm bored today.

Can you feel it?

The crawl under your skin,
bite behind your ear,
claw beneath your jaw.

Irrationality slipping into the brain,
curling between your lobes. Adrenaline
crawling towards you on hands and knees . . .

It feels like the moment before realizing
you may have gone a little *too* far.

THE DIRTY DOG

I'm sorry you died dirty.
It was the first time a dog had made me cry.
I was surprised, but at the same time, I understood why.
This dog died *dirty* and that did not sit right with me.

She came in after her owner noticed her cyst had burst.
She may have had to sit in her own filth for hours.
The smell was awful, and the doctor asked if I would hold
her on the table. The procedure was supposed to be quick.
Everyone knew she wasn't going to make it, all that was left
to do was to give her the last shot she'd ever receive.

But the doctor got busy, several walk ins came at the same time.
An emergency c-section took over all operations
and I sat there with the dirty dog.

I once watched a doctor put a needle into a puppy's chest.
He had only been a couple weeks old, and the signs of parvo
were evident. The needle struck straight into the heart—
we knew because blood entered the tube.
One plunge of the syringe and the medicine ran its course.
I watched as the doctor let go of the needle,
waiting for it to stop bouncing with each beating of the heart.
When it stopped, the puppy was dead.

I didn't cry that day, I was sad, but I didn't cry.

But goddammit if the dirty dog didn't run my heart over with
spiked tires.

She had to wait, with my arms around her, dirty and groaning with
pain,

all for a needle that would end it all.

I wanted so badly to wash her, make her feel better before she died,

but she was heavy, I couldn't lift her on my own,

and the doctor had told me to wait.

There was nothing we could do, we couldn't even clean her,

and we sure as hell couldn't offer her a better wait time.

It just didn't feel right—

making the dirty dog wait for an appointment to die.

I burst into tears while taking her to the freezer.

I kept mumbling,

"I'm sorry. I'm so, so sorry. I'm sorry you had to die dirty.

I'm so sorry you had to die dirty. You should not have died dirty."

I was never even told the dog's name,

but I will never forget the smell, the dullness in her eyes,

or the gentle nudge that she gave me just before

the doctor pushed in the needle,

as if I was the one that deserved to be comforted.

I remember holding your hand
burnt from the stove,
medicine oozing from a metal tube,
worried I'd squeeze out too much love.

Your wrist in my palm . . .
the touch triggered the memory:
Soft hips, smooth thighs—
your skin is silk in my mind
and no words will ever come close
to describing the ache I feel for you.

It's such a beautiful scream, an angelic dream:
reaching out for an experience
I will never reach.
Your hand is the sun, outstretched
to offer a bright, shining lie yet I can't help
but gaze upon you without caution.

I wish we had the chance to be compatible.

It doesn't hurt—
the burn.

I asked for this because I'd rather stare at something I can never have, hold a hand that will never roam where I ache as I squeeze too much medicine from the tube because I'm enamored by pale skin, dark amber eyes watching the too fast rise and fall of my chest—every day, for the rest of my life—than not have you at all.

THE TITLE DOESN'T MATTER FOR THIS ONE

I love the rain—
little drops plopping on my head,
dripping from my brow, spilling on my lashes.
The sight makes you laugh all light and pretty.
I love how cold the water is,
goosebumps rising on my skin,
shivers making me curl into myself.
You wrap your arms around me,
the feeling is warm and soft.
I'm safe here
in the cold rain, the warm love.
You kiss the blush of my cheek
and I make a silent prayer to a dark cloud:
rain every day.

I'M GLAD I FORGOT MY RAIN JACKET

STRANGER

He was dressed in brown and gray—
a monochrome aura blinking in the afternoon light.
My mind was hazy with chemical equations
and letter grades. He knew none of this, only admired
from several feet away. I think I may have scared
him off, probably should have smiled in return.
It's just—well—it's silly.
But I was scared.

He was looking at me and I know, *I know*,
there's no harm in a simple look but he looked
at me like I was worth something. I caught him
the first time—that was coincidence. Second time
I knew for sure. He was looking *at* me.
A stranger, but there he was, staring like I meant
something to him. It scared me.
I didn't feel worth anything.

My mind was hazy, as I said before and I guess
I should have smiled and said hello. If I see him again,
I suppose I will. Just for the hell of it, I'll say,
Hello stranger. Hello again.

HIBERNATION

I crawled under rocks and gravel, feeling the grit rub against my
skin.
Such an interesting sensation to someone who had only felt the sun.
I had spent years in the bright light, my smile glinting under the
rays,
my joy was yellow and green; I bloomed in petals, pollen, and fresh
leaves..
I grew and grew over the years, encouraged by the Sun.
On days when the heat simmered hot and proud,
my skin would singe and turn red.

I was eager, then, for some sort of break, some semblance
of something cooler. But the Sun would beam in protest,
"Enjoy the sunlight! You love the warmth!"
I would stay every time, convincing myself that warmth
would always be both a comfort and a drain.

I was surprised the day I heard a shout from the Earth.
I was completely unaware of the existence of anything
other than the Sun: the warmth, the heat, the burn.
The Sun was angered by the voice distracting me,
and for the first time I realized the Sun is a jealous creature.

The shouts from below did not cease, if anything they grew louder,
and I listened. The Sun hated that I listened.
I could not understand the hot anger, could not understand
why my curiosity was to be regarded with such caution.
One day, my curiosity went too far. The Sun roared in fury
at my resistance— "Look at me! No! At *me!*"

I ran away in fear, my heart in my throat—
far, far away until I reached the end of the Earth and slipped
past the edge.
An eternity passed before I finally fell onto gravel and dirt.
I crawled deep into the Earth. I slithered and squirmed towards
    the voice
who had called for so long unanswered.
All that existed now in my mind was the gritty rub
against my skin and shouting voice bouncing around me.
Just as the sensation became familiar, silence rang.
It was then that I realized my eyes were closed.
I opened them, or so I thought, but saw nothing but darkness.
I paused and tasted its flavor, thinking,
Such an interesting sight for someone who has only ever swal-
    lowed light.

And, suddenly, you appeared from the dark.
I saw your eyes first, glowing with a cool, calm blue.
"Hello, again," you said.
"Again?"
"Of course. Again. You had to begin somewhere.
Can you help me out? I'm afraid I'm stuck."
Your eyes glowed brighter and brighter until the tunnel was coated
in the color. I saw your leg, woven into a tangle of roots.
I tugged and tore at the roots, to no avail.

"What if I can't get you out?" I asked, suddenly very afraid.

"Then we wait."

"But you'll die! You'll die here!"

You chuckled, but I began crying, and you said,

"No, I won't, silly. This is my home. I'm where I'm supposed to be."

I shook my head, not understanding.

"We'll have to wait for the roots to let go in the fall."

"What is fall?"

"A season."

"What is a season?"

"A time of year."

"What is time?"

"Well, what does it mean to you? What would you like to do with time?"

"I just want . . . " I couldn't continue, every thought I'd ever held ended there,

it was always the Sun who ended the sentence.

"That's alright. You don't have to know. Do you want to stay here?"

"I don't want to leave."

"Then don't."

"Is it that easy?"

"Not always."

We settled into a hibernation, and I did not count the hours,

only enjoyed the sound of your voice, the tenderness of your hands,

marveling at the softness touching my burned skin.

You soothed the burn somehow, in a way I never could.

The roots eventually let go. You had to drag me out of the tunnels.

I was so scared, so scared the Sun would burn you into nothing,

take you away from me forever,

But, of course, you were right.

When the dark tunnel faded away into light, I squinted my eyes and gasped.

The sun was so far away, high in the sky, so high it was only a blur of bright.

You smiled at me,

and preceded to show me every season.

SOMETHING WITNESSED AT SUNSET

You're different now.
You just *are*.
Like how you tell me, "*Just breathe. This won't last much longer.*"
It's just *there*.
I'm here, you are there, and this mountain bends
towards the moon begging to grow tall, not broad,
like the pine trees with their spindly branches and straw.
Only mountains don't simply grow, they crumble
as magma eats slowly from the inside out,
gnawing at chunks of rock while air whips
back and forth like sandpaper, grinding the great
mountain down into nothing.
Just like how you tell me, "*Close your eyes and it won't be long now.*"
It's insignificant in the way a mountain
wished to be tall, like the great oaks growing upon it,
but instead it slowly disappeared until there was nothing—
just a hill for a traveler to trip on,
like the stump that makes me fall and skin my knee.
My eyes look up at you, and I see an indifference
settled deep inside.
I see nothing.
Nothing.
In the gaze of someone who once laughed so hard
the landscape paused to grin in contempt.
You.
You who taught me—the emotionless runt—how to love.

I see the depth of your indifference and know
you will never be the same person you once were.
I sigh and erase the old definition, wiping the dirt off my knees,
ignoring the sting of broken skin as best I can.
I hold your hand in mine
and try not to think about how limp the grip is.
It will get better in time. You will heal, just as I once did.

THE EYES OF THE CREEK

Your hands run over me
and all I can think of are
the eyes of the creek—
how those pupils twinkled under the starlight,
the moon winking with each benevolent wave.
You were tender then, too.

    My arms wrap around your waist
    and all I can hear are
    the soft howls of the forest,
    how each note flowed into one another,
    the wind gliding with wondrous wings.
    I was in awe then, too.

        Our gazes catch one another
        and all I can feel is
        the cool damp of the ground,
        how each tendril of grass held a only drop of water,
        the earth breathing into me with chilling affection.
        I was in love then, too. Always will be.

MY RAVEN CAME HOME

I heard my raven pecking on the window last night.
The sound kept me awake till the sunshine scared him away.
I spent half the day talking to the bluebirds, tellin' them,
Get my raven to come home, the front door is open.

The next night came along, rolled in like a season.
My raven pecked at the window, flew away from the glowing horizon.
I felt sorry for him, and I was angry at the bluebirds.
I asked those birds, *Why didn't you tell my raven to come home?*
The bluebirds ruffled their feathers at my accusation,
so I went on to ask the fox for a favor,
Tell my raven to come home, the front door is open.

But the following night, he continued to peck at the window.
Three days with no sleep does no good, none at all.
My body was nailed to the comforter, I slept all through the day,
a nocturnal creature now.

When night rolled back around, I saw my raven rest his skinny
legs on the windowsill. Before he could start pecking,
I flipped the latch and pulled up the windowpane.
He chirped and flew onto my left shoulder, as usual.

I started to get on to him, complain about the pecking,
wanting to know, *Why did you not use the front door as always?*
But I noticed tiny white waves in his eyes.

I'd seen them waves before, in my momma and daddy when they
got old.

So I shut my mouth and ran a hand down my raven's back.

The front door stayed closed, and the window open from then on.

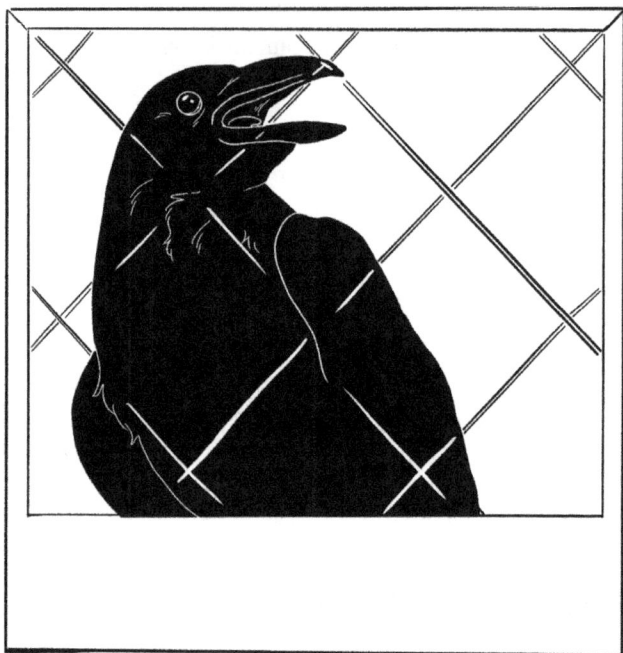

Do you know what it means to heal?   TO HEAL

I used to think healing was the good part,
where you slowly start getting better, feeling better.
But the healing hurts worse than the breaking.
When you're broken,
nothing matters.
Sadness, empathy, feelings don't feel the same,
because you aren't the same.
You are a different entity,
a hollowed-out version of yourself
that cannot be touched and cannot touch.

But to heal—
to heal is to willingly break *again*.
It means sorting out all the pieces, looking at 'em real close
so you can figure out what the hell went wrong the first time.
It all started with one piece—one little piece of the big puzzle
that got turned the wrong damned way.

I remember staring at those pieces for hours,
cheeks stained like glass, eyes burning with salt,
lips bruised by annoyance. I found the problem, of course.
Why it all started happening, the big *"Oh shit, that's it."*
Only I was scared to look at it.
I was terrified to even glance at that ugly, scarred
piece of myself.

Whether I was afraid or not, the piece would remain the same.
Bitter. Familiar. Ominous.
I finally rolled the piece around my tongue,
analyzed the taste and feel of it, felt the burn
deep in my gut when I swallowed.
It hurt like hell, but it was the only way to heal.

You have to look at the ugly bits
and lie. Lie and lie and lie—
telling yourself again and again,
"I am okay with this part of me. This piece is allowed
to exist like all the rest of me."
Eventually, it's not a lie anymore.
You get better. You grit your teeth and heal.

CHARM OF THE SOUTH

It's been a decade since I held her hand,
but I can still feel my baby in the rain.
She rests in the droplets of a Sunday drizzle
making everybody's church clothes wrinkled,
in the thrumming ponds of the trailer park on St. Laurel.
Her rain trickles from the fishing poles stickin' outta
pickup trucks at Piggly Wiggly. She flows down the backs
of hunting dogs, makes the red clay stick to their paws.

My baby and I met in the good ole South,
the kind with pecan pie and fresh catfish,
buttered biscuits that'll make you cry, "Mama!"
and a humid heat that sticks to the skin like jelly.
We had our first kiss at Forest Lake Baptist Church,
right next to the sign reading, "GATOR JERKY SOLD HERE."
And it was next to the wise willow on Boll Weevil Lane
that my baby and I watched the sun rest and rise.

I watch the clouds every morning as I rock
in a peeling wicker chair, right thumb rubbing
at the bumps made from our carved initials.
The smallest blotch of gray cloud makes me squint as I
dig in the garden she planted. It's her dirt keeping
the petals vibrant, vines strong. I've rubbed the silver
off the cross hanging from my neck, nose sniffin' for rain.
Mark my words, the rain will come again soon.

    She always does.

STAY

This. This is why I chose to stay. There is
more to be said, more to be done. More to write.

I've got more smiles to give to a stranger,
and I've still got two hands with room to hold.

I do not fear death and I will not allow those
slender hands to grip me before I've had my fill.

I'm not here to build a career or accumulate
a myriad of medals to clink in a closet.

I want to see a bumblebee fall over a bed
of pollen. I want to taste the honey of life.

Just yesterday, I got to see my brother smile.
It's the fleeting moments that matter the most.

I used to say none of it matters—the kindness
doesn't matter. But life always matters.

I won't lie and say my life got better because
of my decision. But maybe someone's else's life will.

Of course, I say to hell with blind chance.
If agony has the right to scar, so does happiness.

I *can* confidently say that I don't regret my decision. I was worth it, the people around me were worth it.

So don't say hope is gone. Not yet. Because my life hasn't ended—I've got more time to *live*.

If I am to die, let it be in a grave unmarked.
Toss this frozen heap to the mercy of the dirt,
let the thaw be blessed by the boiling sun.

My awakening shall come in the night.
After shovels of clay have suffocated the coffin,
I will rise out of the root infested clog of scorn.

The moon shall kiss this flesh, rotted and alive.
Twinkling stars winking their flirtations,
a yawning sunrise shall reveal the empty slot.

No name, no record, no trace of this grave—
I shall be followed by no one else except:
onyx eyes that laid in watchful stillness,
fixed on the stone, cursing the thick red clay.

She shall follow me through an eager haze,
a body warm and renewed will greet her,
posed open and dew-damp on a blanket of moss.
There, the ground's thick sweat will steam from our
    desire,

An embrace not touched by human or animal,

Nor by light or dark, holy or unholy, king or pawn.

This reunion shall be tender and obscure.

I heal so that I may greet her with worthy hands.

She waits patiently so that she may claim me without restraint.

AVID

Rosary swinging from her neck like the pendulum of a clock,

ticking down, down, down to the taking of my soul's bread.

She has kneaded me over and over again, asking,

> "How much can be mine?"

My mouth becomes an unhinged jaw, dumb and open.

Fogged eyes like glass she bends to breathe upon.

Kneeling, unable to stand on feet made of uncooked dough, I beg,

> "How much can you take?"

I beg for the burn of the oven, yearning for the stain of red blisters

if only to have her kiss the wound and tell me my scars are satisfying.

This is a distasteful route of love, a hurried silence followed by the
wait.

It is in this waiting wake that I turn my head and look when I am
not allowed.

> "Is she watching too?"

I meet her eyes in the shadow of our hereditary rafters.

This house will burn if I ask her.

No matter the strength of my father's glare, her mother's frowning
scorn,

nothing will survive the cataclysmic heat of our lip's embrace albeit
the single utterance:

> "Yes, I've always been watching."

BURN ME, BABY.

A PERSPECTIVE BEYOND THE EYES

Being this sensitive sometimes makes me want
to die right where I stand—
and yet I have so much hope sometimes I think
I'm going to explode.

I feel the pain, yes, I hear the screaming voices
and the wailing cries of the wounded, I feel the pain
of the world and so I also feel

the love and laughter. I feel the life. All I have to do
is close my eyes and listen and I can see the most
beautiful faces smiling in glee, little children being spun
by their parents, an elderly couple laughing at an old wedding
video, two strangers giggling when they can't figure out
how to pass each other in the street, the young fox squealing
as his brother pounces on him from above, a grey dove
cooing at the lonely man in the park.

I see the love of the world and I am reminded of everything
there is to cherish about this existence, this world, however long
it may exist. There is pain, often overwhelming, but the love
can be overwhelming, too, so long as I remember to pause and close
my eyes.

YOU HAVE GOOD BLOOD.

If I could take the colors from the sinking sky
and hand them to you, I would.
If I could fall into the ocean and find your father's body
to give you peace upon my return, I would.
If I could scrub away every scar left on your skin
so you'd never see his hands again, I would.
If I could plunge a knife to my chest, pull out my heart,
suck every drop of blood from my body
to give to you,
I would.

But I can't, and I wish I knew
another way to show you:
This world can be so, so beautiful,
and there are still colors left to discover.
Your father would want you to paint
every shade, and my darling,
your heart is broken now, but not forever.
There is still good blood inside of you.

You're not a failure,
you didn't deserve what happened to you,
and you don't have to apologize
for the time it took you to heal.
I'm not going anywhere.
I love you.

IT'S GETTING LATE,
YOU SHOULD GET SOME REST.

Greetings from the grave you dug,
is the view nice from the balcony I built?
I paid your price, with no will written
for my belongings.
Nice touch, that handwriting,
looked quite convincing
to the judge.

How does it taste? The coffee, that is, you still drink
from the mug I gave you.
How does each tear feel, hot and aching,
as they fall down the cheeks that I once
touched with tender fingertips?
I'm not dead, you know.
At least, not in
your mind.

My voice is still there, still here, whispering
even though you saw my body plunge into the Earth.
Is that why you never visit me?
Because you're afraid that I won't be there?
That, somehow, you'll feel the emptiness
from six feet above?

Fine by me, don't visit, don't talk back.
I'll still chit chat away.
Away, away, away
here to stay, stay,
stay.

> (forgive yourself, will you? What's done is done.
> Let the dead be dead.)

HE WAS KIND.

Try not to abuse what I have given you.
This power was not handed over lightly—
I've made mistakes in the past,
still shake when the wolves howl as a consequence.
I'm afraid of this forest
and yet I love, and I love you,
all because you tell me to trust you
and you haven't given a reason not to.

The love still scares me.
I told you this, and I remember how you sighed,
how you looked at me with a gentle touch
that made me tear up inside.
"I'm sorry no one has ever held you like this before."
You said, arms resting gently on the places exposed.
I don't mean to hurt your feelings
when I tell you not to hit me.
I'm not used to having no need to say it.

Someone once told me there was a target on my skin,
in the way I smiled at strangers,
laughed softly at their greetings.
Softly.
Like how you hold me now,
telling me that I never deserved any of the mistreatment.

. . . you know,
I kinda like how I don't have to tell you what hurts.
You already know that pinches to the skin can bruise,
fingernails can cut, words can break pieces of myself
I struggled to put back together.
I like how you help me.
You help me love each part of myself
and not because you want to take a bite for yourself.

I promise I am doing my best
to believe you when you say,
*"I don't want to hurt you. I love you. I'm never going to intentionally
    hurt you."*
It's nice.
It's soft.
It's a kindness I have given time
and time again, but never felt for myself.
I like how you feel
when you smile because I said, *"I love you."*
I like making you happy.
I like not feeling guilty for asking for your gentle love.
Thank you.

It's the clicking in my neck
as I turn to make sure you're still
glaring at me from across the room
isn't it?
That *click*,
the crank, the grind, the groan
of segments of bone too close together.
Is that what troubles you?
I can't imagine that is your biggest fear,
but the way you refuse to look away from me
tells me so much more than you want me to know.
You worry about me, don't you?

>It's the stillness in the stare
>as I try to find any reason not to trust you.
>Your fingers twitch in anticipation of what I could hand
>>to you.
>Aren't I
>the prettiest thing in the room?
>I gather all the attention from people you never really
>>liked
>and make your confident smile falter in the middle of a
>>sentence.
>Tell me, darling *sweet*,
>is that what angers you?
>Do I remind you of all the things about yourself
>that you like to pretend don't exist? Don't manifest?
>Not so honorable, are we?

It's the tight grip (that isn't yours) on my waist

as I keep my head low, close to the ground, the only solid *thing*.

My teeth biting patterns on the inside of my left cheek—and you appear.

When did you get here? Why are you here? Why pretend to be a knight in shining armor when I have yet to declare danger?

You're acting as if I need to be rescued. I chose to let him touch me, hold me. And I'm not shaking, you are!

All it took was one white lie from your lips, and my night of fun is ruined.

The worst part is, you seem more concerned than angry. Where's the frustration?

Why bother dragging me away from a situation I put myself in?

It's okay, by the way.

I know you aren't taking me home.

I know the gas tank is going to run on empty before you step on the brakes

and I know that you know how much I need this (though I'd never ask).

But, um, I didn't know you were listening . . . when I said

The Holly and The Ivy by George Winston

held a special place within me.

It plays now, over and over, as I watch your hand slide across the steering wheel.

I wonder what else you listened to and how much longer we're going to play this game.

OAK MOUNTAIN

A sneaky salamander winds its way through
sunbaked rocks and splashing water.
Its tiny legs waddle in a frenzy, a thin
vibrant tail flopping behind. Its body
squeezes in between two stones, yellow
eyes close and open at the smallest
of sounds until the heaviness makes
the salamander weary.
It falls asleep to the lullaby of the waterfall.

Skin warms beneath a summer sun, your stare like a fox,
watching and waiting for a moment to strike. I pull the smoke
of your joint into my lungs as if the wisps are sacred rites. "Go
jump in the water!" I laugh, catching the sharpness in your pupils

like a child holding a knife. You surprise me when you step out
of your cover-up, your expression grim and I almost ask
you to stop. "It was just a joke!" I want to say, like a circus
clown trying to stop a kid from crying. But the splash

flicks my worries into the water. You float like an island
that moves with the wind, never touching the creek floor.
"How's it feel?" I ask. Your back is to me. "Like a fridge,
it's cold as hell." Two seconds pass before I sprint for the dark
water, ignoring your protests. I leap, changing my shape
to form a cannonball. *Splash!* I sink—the water a window

to an alternate reality of fish and snapping turtles. I listen
to the creek's voice, admire the way it folds and makes
a gentle roar I could fall asleep to. You pull me up, the change
in atmosphere is jarring and then you say, "I'm in love with you."

PAPER AND PAINT

She knew she was made of paper
and so she knew she'd have to prove she
was capable of holding ink, paint, ash, oil—
"Make yourself the prettiest canvas in the room,"
Her mother used to say, pearls shining in the sun,
"and no man will be able to resist you."
Her mother was a liar.

All girls are made of paper and in
grade school they are taught how to
keep themselves clean while the boys learn
how to be artists, how to make things dirty,
how to make a profit off of the artwork.
Every night she would dream of what it must
feel like to make a blank space colorful.

She soon found that men didn't care if she
was a blank face or a smiling sunrise,
because men don't need a reason to paint when
they're told permission has already been granted.
She stared at paintbrushes and markers until
the colors were all a blur. The day she finally
made the first stroke of yellow, red, and blue
           she became an artist.

Little adventure, will you wait for me?
I'm not finished packing.
I have to prepare, I have to wait
because there's people here, you know that!
I can't just up and leave!
Don't look at me with scrutiny, I'm doing my best.
I'm giving this a chance, I am!
It's just taking time. *Needed* time. Reasonable time.
But I'm working on my dreams.
So will you wait for me?
Wait for my courage to catch up
with my imagination?
I promise not to forget you,
just don't leave me behind.

LITTLE ADVENTURE

CAREFUL–

Silence, my darling, takes shelter in these woods.
The trunk of each tree holds an ache,
flocks of birds wide as the great lakes
block sight of the pines.

Have you ever fallen?
Not from a lift in the pavement, but fallen
down a cliff's ledge, eyes locked on death,
the scythe waiting patiently at the rocks below.
Just as you wonder if the falling will ever end,
it does.
Abruptly. Swift.

Pain, my darling, lingers here,
in the fearful hearts of each thumping hare,
the trembling hooves of each white deer,
in the final breath of each howling wolf who
lost the battle of hunger.
The winter is cold,
and though your hands are so warm in mine,
I am still afraid.
(*But I trust you. I will always trust you.*)

FRIENDLY GLANCES

I'll stop loving you one of these days, right?
I bet you'll make a snarky comment with light-hearted intentions—
it'll sting enough that I don't laugh.
You know me too well,
and yet not enough sometimes.
Too comfortable with my vulnerabilities,
too familiar with wounds that never healed.
Maybe my love will fade because
you'll say something stupid—
something selfish and conceited.
If that's the case, you'll probably be deep in thought,
one leg hanging off the chair,
the other held against your arm.
Your double chin will show, I'll notice a pimple on your forehead—
and that'll be it.
I'll realize I'm not attracted to you in that way.
We—are—just—friends.

But friends don't fantasize about lips on their shoulder, a fleeting memory I would never dare forget no matter how long I deny my love. No matter how long I deny that you've never really hurt my feelings. You've never meant me any harm. You know me well enough, too much maybe, but you also know too little. Notice too little. Probably a good thing. I confess too much with my lingering eyes and long, stubborn smile.

Whatever, anyways.

Friends can love double chins, right? Friends can fall in love with each knuckle, the bend of the knee. Every scar, every mole. Friends can wish they had the time to count each mark that makes up the skin they want to touch. Friends can crave a warmth that doesn't come from the body. Really, really close friends can love every piece.

We are just friends.

That's why you kissed my shoulder.

That's why I trace the same spot over and over at two am.

STAY HERE.

Violent enterprise breaks your skin,
    tears you into pieces so when you look in the mirror
        someone else is smiling there, taunting you, daring you to
            stare back.
            Can you still feel it? The sun? Are we too far gone to feel
            the warmth?
I think we can make it. I think that
    if we hold onto one another and make a promise
        not to look into that mirror, we will make it out of this.
            So, stay here, baby, stay with me. Look at me, look into
            my eyes
                that adore every part of you and would never ask
                you to change.
We can build the steps one by one.
    Sometimes when I look at the stars, I swear I can
        see them wrinkle in distaste at what they see below.
            But when I kiss the moonlight and prove I am capable
            of love
                that wrinkle loosens, and I know, I just know there's
                still a chance.
I still love you, even like this and I cannot imagine
    a world where we don't stay with one another, so please
        listen to me when I say there are outside forces rooting for us.
            There are people who think you are so beautiful, they
            would devote
                their whole life if only to see you smile, a true and
                pure smile.
                I would do that. You know that, right?

Your skin is raw and red, but I am here with bandages,
	ready to heal you the second you give me permission to touch you.
		This place is hard on creatures like you because you care
			more than others.
			But I . . . I don't want you to go yet. I need you here and
				I'm sorry that I do.
					It's selfish to ask you to stay, but can't you? If I
					am here, can you

						stay?

TO TOUCH

I love how it feels to touch
people when they are
touching back.
Not the sideways glance
at the grocery store,
or the half hazard nod
that hardly recognizes
either person's cognitive
consciousness.
I love the awkward handshake
that turns into a bear hug,
the confident smirk that
shatters into an ugly cackle,
the hand that touches clothed thigh
and plays with the seam of fabric
along the edge.
It's the touch that breaches
the space we perceive as reality,
history repeating itself
in that funny little wrinkle of time.
To touch and be touched back.

NICE

He said,
"Show me your face."
He held out both hands,
stared at me with
curious vulnerability.
I asked with sarcasm,
"Are you sure you have
the time?"
Not expecting an answer,
I began removing the pins
holding up my smile.
I unstitched my widened eyes,
pulled away strings
in my cheeks,
and unhooked the
tilt of my tone.
"Hello," he said,
"It's nice to finally meet you."
I couldn't help but question,
"Is it? Do you truly find this
entertaining?"
He merely chuckled.
"Who told you that you
have to be entertaining?"
I had no answer.
"It is nice," he said.
For whatever reason,
I believed him.

JUST SCARED

You're analyzing pieces
I didn't even know I had.
You're taking apart my
insecurities and calling
me beautiful and lovely
and your hand in mine
feels like that one
Fourth of July
before my grandpa died.
I feel like I've seen you
before in the blank spaces
of my bedroom ceiling.
I'd stare at the dull corners
and tell myself eventually
something would happen
to make all the pain feel
better. And yet, you've
cured me of nothing.
Instead you're proving to
me that all this time I
wasn't sick, just scared.

DISTANCE

The day you didn't touch me, I fell in love with you.
I noticed that you have more freckles on your left cheek
than your right. You've got a habit of scrunching your nose
right before you start laughing, and every time you enter a room
your eyes scan back and forth, taking in all the faces, shapes and
    colors
surrounding you.
I fell in love with the distance between us, because for the first time
    in my life,
I felt safe in the presence of a man. I don't know what you saw in
    the first moments
that we met, whether it be the flinch in my smile, the hesitation in
    my movements, or the
cowering of my shoulders—but somehow, you knew. You knew
    that I needed the distance
in order to feel safe. I kept waiting for you to disappoint me with a
    misogynist joke or hard stare,
but you never did.

I was just another person, another one of those faces in the crowd
that happened to catch your eye. And while many men would see
    the distance
as a nuisance, an inconvenience at best—you saw it as an opportu-
    nity to show kindness.

The day I will never forget, the day you didn't touch me, didn't get
    within three feet of me—
I fell in love.

ALLIGATOR WOMAN

Alligator Woman,
who first told you of the scales
on your skin?
It is written that a man
discovered you here, deep in the swamp.
Is this true?
When he first laid eyes
on you, blonde hair brushed by a cloud
of smoke and glory,
did his stare feel warm
or cold?

Tell me, Alligator Woman,
did you know you were being hunted?
Or did you think he could be a friend?
It must be so lonely in the swamp.
No one to keep you company except
the biting midges and soft bellied trout.
Some people claim you were born out of mud
and slime. Some say you were once a snake,
but the gods punished you for your slender body
and forked tongue. You were made
into this—
a creature whose smile makes the water wither.
Every time you snap a branch you hear its echo
and are reminded of how isolated and alone
you truly are.

Tell me, Alligator Woman,
am I really such a surprise?
I'm sorry the man found you first.
I'm sorry you were punished for existing.

If you'd like,
I'll count your scales and tell you
why each one is special.
I'll teach you how to enjoy your smile,
how to live for yourself, how to love
yourself.

Alligator Woman,

did you know you have the loveliest yellow eyes? Like dandelions.

TALL BOY WITH A BIBLE

You've always been so fond
of your little wooden workshop.
You carve and carve with precision
and confidence, bringing me all the pieces
in search of verbal praise and eyes dipped in awe.
I wonder if you'll try to carve yourself
out of the coffin you've been building
since the day we married. I think you'll try.
And I think you'll lose.
I know you'll lose.
I've seen you holding *her* picture,
knuckles white with the grip.
White like bone.
White like the teeth
of the teenage girl grinning
at the camera.
I haven't looked that young in years,
because I'm not supposed to, you knew
when you married me—
I'm your mother.
And you—the little boy
hiding inside of a preacher,
shouting from the pulpit
and sneaking into church
any day but Sunday
to touch someone who does not belong to you.
But what do really you want? To own her?
Do you want to give her my diamond ring?

Stalker, Creeper, Whittler, Preacher.

Why don't you whittle yourself another wife?

This one is tired of wiping your mouth

and changing your diaper.

Preacher, Lover, Husband, a man who needs a lawyer—

I've followed the orders of a man my entire life.

God, Preacher, Public Speaker, Man with a microphone.

Just enough charisma and charm

to make the crowd go wild when you wave the Bible

and point your finger at a red statue of thorns.

You carved it yourself, after all.

Carved me, too.

Your love has always been quieter than your cruelty.

But these divorce papers

pictures of messages sent, pictures of *her* . . . loud. Loud. Loud!

You're breathing and I don't know why.
It's more than just the hospital lighting,
or the bubble of blood bobbing in your IV tube
or dip of dark bags under your eyes.

I came to the hospital to tell you goodbye.
To finally put my *dear* father to rest.
So why did your finger twitch when I got here?
Why did the heart monitor skip a beat when I spoke?

The nurse tells me you can still hear me.
'Even in a coma!' she cheered. As if there were
something to be celebrated. I bet you didn't tell them
about your drinking habits. Or your smoking ones.

But I bet the doctors still know. How could they not?
A few scans will show the truth: a stroke wasn't the only
thing that could kill you. It could have been your first wife,
your second wife, your ever lovely daughter that you won't
recognize.

It's been a while. Maybe that's why—I watch your chest
move up and down and up and down. I no longer
recognize you.
Maybe that will make you feel better. If you wake up.
I think . . .

*I miss you. I'm afraid of this man in the hospital bed because he used
to tuck me in. He used to sing me bedtime stories and kiss my fore-
head goodnight. I ate his homemade cheddar poppers with a shovel,*

got a tummy ache every time he made them. He was there for my first steps, first trophy, first love, first heartbreak, first rebellion.

I'm afraid of you, dad. Dead or alive, I'm afraid.

THE DISAPPOINTMENT.

CRACKED GLASS

Does it hurt to know I'm never going to *not* flinch?
Tell me, with your arms wrapped around me—
does this part hurt?
Is it love?
There's a *tug* in my chest every time I stare
at the soft pink of your lips, wondering
how many flowers mimic the color and yet
never come close to the shade that attracts
me so much I'm almost scared of this—of us.
And then there's a different tug—one that pulls
when I least expect it, pulls so hard it hurts and I think:
Why does this feel like heartbreak when I am so, so
in love with the person in front of me?
Is love *supposed* to hurt this much?
Do I care? Do I even care when it means
that I get to hold you?
I'm not asking because I want an answer, but
because I need one.
I have to have one if I am to continue loving you.
I have to, baby.
Sometimes when you touch the invisible
wounds on my skin, I *flinch* and so do you.
My wounds hurt the both of us.
So don't lie to me, baby—
am I a blessing or a burden?
Am I good enough to keep when it hurts?

SOMEONE SENT YOU ROSES!

I still know what you are.
The floral scent of your smile isn't strong
enough to mask your violence.
I stare at the red roses with no thorns
sitting pretty in a glass vase on my kitchen table.
I bet you spent all night chopping off every thorn,
carefully peeling away the flower's natural defense.
How kind of you to send me roses—a gentle
reminder of what you are capable of.

I caress the silky, crimson petals
and I remember.

A knife glints beside the vase.
I see a small sliver of green,
and I remember what it felt like
to be the red that seeped
onto that metal blade.

I would kiss you anywhere, anytime
but I can't tell you that so instead
I count the stars while you count
my breaths because you're always
watching me when I'm not watching
you and I can't help but stare when
you aren't looking. We've both
convinced ourselves we are content
with the tense silence, but there's violence
in this quiet surrounding us, darling—
I can't hold on much longer pretending
the hand on my thigh isn't burning
like a fire that we both lit without
meaning to.

I don't regret the flames. I don't regret
the burn as you kiss my cheek goodnight,
or the heat curling in my chest every time
you stare at me one second too long.

Darling, if you're ready, let's not waste
another moment—
watch me while I burn. Tell me how much
you love me, how you really love me, tell
me about the places you've been aching to reveal.
I am yours to adore—revealed fully by your flame.

STOP PRETENDING YOU DON'T WANNA
TOUCH ME

PERSUASION OF THE MIND

Is your imagination like mine?
Can you shift the world around you?
Can you make your body tingle like sparkling
water? I'm curious to know how this feels
to someone else—leaving the body
and entering the mind.

I've always felt one step away from losing it all.
My sanity, my life, my entire existence—
it could all go away in an instant. I don't mind.
If anything, the thought is refreshing. If I can disappear
in a single moment, the pain can disappear too.
All the pain and agony,
no matter how overwhelming—
is not invincible.

I tend to live life with one foot in the future,
the other teetering in the past. My delusions
sometimes feel more real than what's right
in front of me. Do you ever feel the same?
Have you ever stared at a window long enough
for the glass to disappear? Ever touched the skin
on your body and felt something other than skin?
Or seen figures that hide in the corner of your eye,
but never in plain sight? Have you ever walked
into a room and wondered,
am I dreaming?

The other day I took a stroll in the woods. I listened
to the sounds of creaking pine branches, fluttering cardinals,
and squirrels scratching their way up the sycamore tree.
I stared at this world around me, and the strangest
thought came to mind:

Delusion or reality, I am fond of this existence.
If I can warp reality enough that I can hardly tell
the difference, what else do I have control over
that I previously convinced myself otherwise?
How can I use this to my benefit, or the benefit
of those around me? If anything is possible in
this world that I have created,
what would I like to see change?

THE PRODIGY

I want to rip my talents to shreds like the dog I am.
I want to bark at the sun until my voice is broken and raw,
run back and forth across a track of concrete until my legs fold.
My hands are young and valuable—dare me to chop one off?
This skin—it is soft, smooth, malleable—how about some texture?
Compliment my smile and I'll pull each tooth out one by one.
I don't want to be pretty, I don't want to be *wanted*.
The day I become useless is the day I become free.

I have become exactly what I was taught to hate
and I couldn't be happier. It's fun to have nothing to offer.
No one gets to pick the parts they are born with,
but I've grown to be an accomplished mechanic.
I love to see eyes rolling in my direction, a snark comment
close behind. Conflict gives opportunity to question—
and boy do I *love* to question everything. But most of all,
I love proving that I have a mind of my own with no
intention of following a path to exploitative "*success*".

I'd rather have a legacy of good times and bruises
than your last name. Got it?

THE SPEECH THAT SAVED OUR MARRIAGE

Come on, can't we just yell for once?
I got a face full of tears, snot in my nose
and your shirt is not even wrinkled.
Why are you so scared to have flaws?
I keep walking in the house with muddy
feet and there's a stain on every blouse I own.
You've got a label for everything
and I've never seen you angry.
I'm not stupid, but I was, and so I
boxed up all the hurt and the pain,
shoved it in a closet and hoped I'd be fine.
But, baby, the wounds aren't in the feeling,
they're bleeding inside you. How long
are you going to hide a wounded heart?
If you want to please me so badly,
look at yourself in the mirror and *swing*!
Feel the glass breaking, feel your knuckles
sting and know the feeling will pass.
Let yourself cry, let yourself wash the wound
before you wrap it up this time.
When you're done, I'll be here waiting
to kiss the scars, new or old, for better or for worse.

JUST HIBERNATING

I'm not dead yet, darling, just hibernating.
You see I decided to walk into the woods
late one night. The moon was full,
I felt empty and I couldn't help but wonder
how the moonlight would taste mixed
with midnight air. I crave flavors
you've never understood, but you tried
to feed me best you could. But, darling,
there's more to life than giving away
pieces of yourself. There's more than legacy.

In the dark of the wood, I found myself
frightened. Skin cooled and wet from
fear, sweat trickling down a wrinkle
in my spine. I followed a voice,
familiar and strange and far away.
I followed the fear, pulled it closer
like a string of web. Fear reminds
me of honey—sticky, sweet,
and glowing. It's a beautiful feeling
when you lean into it.

My whole life, I've been too scared
of being uncomfortable. I built myself
a box, gave myself a label so I was easy
to identify, to find. So when everyone
and anyone needed me, I was there even
when I had nothing left to offer. I sat on
the ledge of this reality I had built, and
when I stayed perfectly still and listened—
there was no one clapping in the audience.
I put myself in a movie and pretended it was real.

I laid on the damp moss of the forest
floor, closed my eyes and dreamed
I was drinking the moonlight. I tasted
starlight and darkness and *fear*.
I tasted something real.
I'm not dead yet—just hibernating.
Thinking of the fearful flavor over and over
until I learn the lesson. Until I can
confidently say:
I'm not afraid of my fear anymore.

TO BE CONTENT

Fondness is the pizza sauce smeared on her cheek—
the fork she grips in her fist, lifting high into the air
as she exclaims, *"Loneliness is the heart of consumption!*
And dinner cannot be eaten without dessert!"
I know I am in love, but even if I didn't,
I would be still.

Eagerness is the button on my bathroom floor, torn
during a morning make out that started with a
spilled cup of coffee. The cup is still sits on the
counter, a hazel ring dried up on the inside.
I know I should probably put it away, but I
decide to leave it out for a couple more days.

Sadness is the reason I finally say, *"I love you."*
Snot is coming out of my nose, but you laugh
and tell me how foolish we both are. Victims
to time and ignorance, too busy convincing
ourselves that there's another day around the
corner to notice that Goodbye has already
arrived. You kiss me and walk away.

On his deathbed, David Hume said
it was "a most unreasonable fancy
that we should exist forever."
I repeat this to myself, watching another
airplane fly past my window. Part of me
fully believes you are on that plane,
looking down at me somehow.

I find that in this moment, I am
fond of your memory,
eager for your return,
sad at your absence,
and content that everything has its end.

THE HUNT

I'm fascinated by you, Hunter.
At first, I thought your name betrayed you.
The hand that beckoned me closer was not
      a hand familiar with a knife, bow, rifle.
Your eyes were absent of the fog lingering in
      the eyes of those who've taken life.
I could not imagine amaryllis red lips whispering
      the prayers of grace over a dying doe's body.
I was not frightened by your touch. The only chills
      I felt were caused by lust and lust alone.
Round cheeks and a soft belly entrancing me with
      every movement.
Your very breath beguiled me, and then I realized:
      Prey knows how to survive.
The greatest hunt of all:
              the one you aren't aware of.
Now I don't even care. Eat me.
      Pierce my flesh with a silver arrow.
Run your hands over every part of me.
      Bend over me and whisper a prayer
            detailing everything you're going to do.
My body is yours to devour.
But, Hunter, I hope you haven't forgotten—
      half the fun is in the *chase*.

MODEST GIRL

I feel his hands and I know that I am in danger.
On the table rests a golden cross and a set of pearls,
I ask myself, "*Which one will keep me safer?*"

I am dressed and ready for the day, my body
is my own and I feel safe in it. He hands me a coat.
I feel his hands and I know I am in danger.

The air is bitter but turns sweet when I swallow.
I look into a shop window, at the blouses on display.
I ask myself, "*Which one will keep me safer?*"

Modesty is honesty with one's self-respect. If this is true,
why is he staring at me? Why am I the one to feel shame?
I feel his hands and I know I am in danger.

I cannot seem to decide if my own perception or other's
perception of myself matters more. Who's to say when
I ask myself, "*Which one will keep me safer?*"

Modesty is trust in one's self-respect. Trust is believing
his sincerity. Self-respect is the taser or the pepper spray.
I feel his hands and I know I am in danger.
I ask myself, "*Which one will keep me safer?*"

HYDRA

I have created an ache
for that which I cannot
have.

Dangle in front of me,
sweet angel of death.
Taunt me so that I may
come to realize my
mistake.

Whisper in my ear
a language that I will
only understand half of.

Make me regret each
step I take away from you,
make me change my mind,
even if it means
putting my own happiness
before yours.

You'll be happier
without me,
this I am sure of.
But without you—

I will never be able to
forget the way your
eyes grew in hunger
as you stared at me
and not him.

RETURN LABEL & RECEIPT

I usually flick fear off my shoulder like a flea,
but *you* darling, dressed in a wrinkled tee
and baggy shorts—terrify me.

My heart has twisted into a big buzzing bee,
bones unfurling to form little gems that I hope will please you,
muscles making honey goo so I'm sweet when you bite.

Aren't my eyes pretty from this angle?
Aren't I a precious doll you'd like to grab the neck of?
Pathetic and terrified—I am reminded of why I must continue
replacing nuts and bolts, turning tight with tools
I don't know the names of, palms bleeding blisters
just to make another crank.

A beautiful beast you are to whisper in my ear why
I have to finish fixing what life has broken.
But look dear! I'm all done!
I read the manual and put all the parts back together!
Does this anatomy please you?
I'll be sitting on the shelf at the mega mart
waiting to be bought with pretty kisses and paper hearts.

TALK

Your voice sounds different,
did you know that?
It's only been a few months,
but I didn't recognize the person
on the other end of the phone.

You apologized.
You've never done that before—
not without a finger crossed behind your back.
I had dreaded the call, expecting a tantrum.
I'd put on dad's cap and mom's perfume
read the script that I didn't believe in
hoping you'd understand the language still.

I didn't have to do any of that, though.
You weren't mad, not even a little.
"Only if you can. I understand if you can't."
Well, that's certainly new.
I'd be lying if I said I wasn't elated.
I would also be lying if I said
I trusted a word you said.

Pleasant tone or not—
you're trying, I'll give you that.
It's just—
the cut is still fresh
and someone asked about the bandage yesterday.

WHY DON'T YOU WHINE A LITTLE LOUDER?

If that smirk gets any bigger,
I'm gonna pull the fucking trigger.
Narcissistic baby, tell me what it feels like
when someone tells you
"No."

Go ahead and roll your eyes.
I'll just keep sharpening this knife,
with an eye on that heart
holding sticky blood inside,
making each pump go
"Flick! Flick! Flick!"

No, that machine doesn't work quite right,
always had a few gears gone.
I wonder who pulled them out? Did you think
you didn't need them? Did you think you could
cheat the system?

Narcissistic baby,
tighten that fist and let it fly.
Give me one more reason to finish this fight
that started the day I was forced to share
oxygen with you.

Does my blank face anger you?
My lack of reaction shows
what I want you to know:
You're nothing but a baby
who has never been told "No."

Your tricks are old to me.
I've seen it all.
If you continue to speak to me
that way, this blank face
may fall apart.

Don't make up a mirror to flip,
hell, even your mother agrees—
you are the Narcissistic one,
baby.

MENELAUS BLUE MORPHOS

Yelling at the lamp in the living room
because the bulb is brighter than the blue
in your eyes, and I can still remember how
they shined. My menelaus blue morphos who
fluttered to rest in my palms, tiptoed on the edge
of my cheek. I'd told my butterfly I loved her.
I loved her when she could fly and I loved her when
she couldn't.

Yet even now I can't control the irrational anger
that makes the fake fluorescents offensive.
It's not your fault, baby. How could you have seen
the spider's web in the moonless night?
Parts of you are still there, blinking blue caught in the strings.
You crawl so you can still rest on my shoulder,
but the blue, my baby blue—is gone.
I hope I will meet her again someday.

CIRCLE DRIVEWAY

I was ready to dig you outta that grave—
that stupid pit of dirt your children dug.
I was ready to ride a coffin straight down
into hell. I was ready to sneak you away,
to trade places so that you'd get your chance.
You deserved it. If there's anything in this life
you deserved—it was a single goddamned chance.

I remember us sitting on your Daddy's back porch.
We munched on pecans, I vented about unfairness
while you preached on how to be resourceful. Notice
how I don't say grateful—you never thanked God
for being cruel, but you did know how to make use
of what you had. It didn't matter when you were
kicked out at sixteen, pregnant and alone. You made do.

I helped when you let me, which wasn't often.
Were you trying to set an example? Trying to prove
to your daddy you weren't a "degenerate whore"?
Or was there something you wanted to prove to yourself?
I can say you proved one thing—nothing would ever
keep you down. Even when life never gave you a chance to fully heal.
I guess that's what I'm angry about. You never got to live.

People love giving out trophies to the poor and unfortunate.
Wealthy folks who pretend they aren't that wealthy
watch crime TV shows and think of how strong and worthy

the single mother working three jobs is while she struggles
to soothe her wailing toddler. People shouldn't pity her.
If they really cared, they'd be angry. They'd be so angry
their hearts would burn into nothing but hot, black ash.

You're nothing but ash now. But you were always so much
more. You could've been so much more if you had just
been given an opportunity. Just one measly piece of luck
and you would have made an empire. Instead, you spent
your life exhausted, giving your children everything
you never got. You gave your life so they could have a future.

I have a theory: in your next life—cus' I bet God is gonna
give you another—you will be born in a nice suburban home
with rose bushes and a circle driveway and a whole room just for
    games.
You're going to get that chance. You're going to build a goddamned
    empire.

THE COFFEE SHOP

Wait, don't go yet. I remember you.
Somewhere, we knew each other's hearts.
You've felt my touch before, I know it,
and I recognize the scent of your soul:
lavender, lilac, and warm cinnamon.
Why did we hold eye contact for so long?
If you're a stranger, then the sky is green.

Truth refuses to appear to me, but I know
my intuition. I trust my visions. This may
sound like some kind of insanity,
but just think of the implications. Think
of reasons for why we stepped into the shop
at the exact same time, turned heads, locked eyes,
and drew in a hard breath. Your eyebrows lifted
and your lips fell apart.

Such a silly, fragmented moment. Broken because
you blushed and darted away like a scared
mouse. I can't blame you much because I feel
like a mad man. But I was sane before all this,
so I have hope I may be sane some time after.
Perhaps if I see you again. I don't want to be a creep.
I walk out of the shop emptyhanded, I've always
been a coward. Can you blame a man for running?

Halfway down my street, my phone buzzes.
A follow request on Instagram. I recognize you immediately.

THE ANGEL AND THE DEVIANT

Sap on your cheek, cherry blossoms
in your hair—could you get any more
perfect? Jesus, and your eyes are sparkling
in a way that says you could eat me at any
moment. Should I be worried, baby?

We've got another mile to hike to the car,
not sure if I'll make it before you try
to break my inner do-gooder. It's funny,
honey, because I think you do this only
to irritate me as gently as possible.

You control your inner deviant some,
I'll give you that. But let's be honest—
you've always been self-indulgent.
I love that about you. And yet by some
miracle we have made it to the car with
no transgressions. I'm proud and disappointed.

I pull out of the parking lot. I realize my mistake.
The glint in your eyes had turned to fire,
and my hands were occupied with the wheel.
Lord help me.

I AM NO PERFORMER

If no one is watching . . . do I exist?
Do I matter if there are no eyes on me?
I'd like to believe that I do. I've come
to the realization that believing is all
I really need to be true.
If I believe in myself, I exist.
If I do not believe in myself, I sit
in purgatory. Waiting like an embryo
floating inside its mother's belly.
The belief in myself must be born again.

I cannot depend on other people to provide
my own humanity. I must give it to myself
by believing that I deserve it.
I deserve to exist, whether I am being watched
or left purely to my own devices.
I need no audience.

My existence is not a performance.
It is an experience.
I can share my experience,
though I am the only one who can touch it.

I am an experience.
I am ever-changing and undefinable.

I have awareness, feelings, consciousness—

I exist.

TWO WEEKS AFTER I STOPPED TAKING BIRTH CONTROL

I had gone several months without
feeling anything. So when the laughter touched me—
I was shocked.

I sat in the movie theater, still as a rock
yet more alive than I had been
in months.
I could feel the *laughter.*
I could feel the joy emanating
from the people around me.
Another funny quip from the side character,
more chuckles arise in the dark room.

I breathe and suddenly there's air in my lungs.
There's air and there's light and people
and I can touch all of it.

I was so overwhelmed and overjoyed,
I had to hide my tears behind a quiet smile.

I just couldn't stop crying because after going
so long being so numb . . .

I had forgotten what laughter sounded like.

I had forgotten how it bounces back and forth,
how one beat of laughter clashes into the following,
the beautiful bellows from deep in the belly
and the silent slapping of the knee . . .

IN THE MOMENT

Dear world, leave me be to heal.
Let me finish sewing together
the bits of me cut open by tragedy
and guilt. I'm coughing on the smoke,
too busy chasing my own self doubt
to realize there was a fire blooming
in the oven.

Bleeding, coughing and choking ain't
no fun. But these things are just symptoms.
That's what I tell myself while I finish
my stitching up of myself.
Ah! There I am. Freshly cleansed,
ready to dirty myself up again.

That's what life is, right? Part of life
is learning what it means to be clean
again just to go right back into the mud.
You finish scrubbing at the same time
you forget why you were scrubbing
in the first place.

I've come to terms with this fact of my life.
I am overjoyed by the possibilities.
Watch me go up and down, left and right
and back again because I can be knocked
down but I cannot be forced to stay.

You can't hold onto a fog.
I am mist. I am never a solid thing
because I am an ever-changing thing.

So leave me be, for now.
Come back tomorrow and maybe
I'll be ready for conversation.
Right now I am too busy existing.

UGLY

Today I choose to be an ugly thing.
I want to be worthless to the world
that demands sacrifice, begs for a martyr
it doesn't deserve. Where is the value
in sacrament? Where is the value in purity?

I've gotten to the point in life
where I'm tired of it.
Go away.
Leave me be. Let me rot.
I will not be your martyr.
I will not be the worker that drags herself
till there's nothing left of her own humanity.
I define the meaning of my own life.

Don't tell me one path is the only way.
Wake, eat, work, sleep, repeat.
"Give yourself away and you will be gifted
everything you ever wanted!"
Your pretty profit offends me.
Disgusts me.

I don't want the money.
I don't want the success.
Our definitions differ.
I wish to be content, happy, well-rested.
I want to exist.

A CHANCE

This. This is the feeling that told me to run last time.
I'm still healing from last time. Still coddling the hurt.
This is a feeling of red flags and dark hallways.
It's eerie and hollow and heavy all at the same time.
I promised myself I'd *never* ignore this feeling again.
So
tell
me
why
I
can't
stop
running
towards
you.

(for change)

TO DAD

I watch a bumblebee cling to a flower,
swinging to and fro in the wind on a floral seesaw—
and I feel your love.
I stare up at the night sky, cheeks warm
and sticky with summer's humid kiss. A star winks—
and I feel your love.
I giggle at a pun, the laughter is a cloud of light,
joy bubbling like a carbonated drink inside of me—
and I feel your love.

I feel you in the splashes of water at the creek,
in the warmth that comes from late night conversations,
in the twinkling fireflies roaming around the underbrush.

No matter how far away I may be,
I know I will always see you in the patterns
of life whizzing past me every day.

It's difficult to comprehend the idea of eternal,
unconditional love but you make it a lot easier.

I love you, Dad.
Thank you for being you and thank you
for always showing your love in ways big
and small.

NEON ANGEL

You're hypnotic when you touch me,
eyes glowing lilac-green, a neon-angelic
form come down from the heavens to disarm
me in the gentlest way possible. You use sneaky
tactics, but I don't blame you.
I taunted you first.
The subtle touches to your skin, pretty smiles
pointed in your direction—
I had this gun cocked and ready long before
you knew who I was.
Yet now, as your hands map out the curves
of my body, lips brushing against flushed skin—
I don't feel beaten.

I feel aflame, akin to the artificial, gut coiled
and twisted in patterns unlike the human species.
You're changing me internally.

Many have touched the skin you now caress,
none allowed to stay more than one night.
But *you*—

You can take me. Wherever you like. However you please.

THE DAY I LEFT MY DREAM

I was crying while stirring what would be dinner.
Probably got tears in the pan. I didn't care.
All I could think of was the soul of that dog . . .
I hoped she was dead.

The day started out bad, so at least I had a heads up
things were gonna go south soon. What I didn't
know was that shift at Bryant Denny Veterinary Hospital
would be my one of my last. I was working as an assistant,
to be tech of sorts. I did a little bit of everything,
but nothing too complicated.

The first thing I saw was Daisy. She was lying on her side,
a thin blanket wrapped around her. I could see there was
wrapping and gauze on her leg. She had several open wounds
around her body. I was told that wild dogs had attacked her
a couple nights before. I wondered why she wasn't brought
in sooner.

Later that afternoon, I learned that the owner had lied.
The vet called after looking over Daisy's condition
and recommended euthanasia as the most humane choice.
Daisy would, unfortunately, not recover. The owner disagreed,
however, and revealed that he had taken Daisy to a veterinarian
a week prior and received the same recommendation.

I was horrified. This poor dog had these wounds for more
than a week. All that suffering . . . for what? I understood
the owner's hesitance to say goodbye, but I was angry.
I was angry and then I was livid when I pulled back the blanket
so we could transport her to the truck.

Her entire leg had rotted. I'd never seen muscle so gray.
Her skin was green and she shook like she was frost-bitten.
I sank to the ground. I couldn't do it. I couldn't touch her.
Another vet came in and asked for my assistance.
Another co-worker took my place.

The vet needed me to hold a cat for euthanasia.
Apparently, the cat was very old, and the time
had come. Why prolong the suffering? When I picked
her up, she was barely six pounds. Her blonde fur was thin
and greasy. I could see in her eyes that she was tired.
I wrapped her up in a blanket; the vet and I walked to the car.

The owner was a sweet woman. She had a kind voice as she tried
to hide her sadness for the sake of the moment. She gave the kitty
a couple rubs on her head, the vet asked me to hold for the needle,

and as soon as the shot was done, the cat switched. She turned on
    her
owner, scratching her hand and arm. We scrambled to get the cat
    under
control, trying to be gentle as possible. I felt so sorry for the owner.
There were tears in her eyes as I pulled away. A kind moment,
    soured.

As I moved away, I looked over at the other vehicle in the parking
    lot.
The truck. Two techs in green uniforms were putting Daisy into
the backseat. She never cried out in pain, just laid limp.
I looked down at the cat. She wasn't breathing.

So I was crying in my dinner. I knew I could never be
a veterinarian. If I had to make decisions like that? Allowing
an innocent, suffering animal to be forced to live just for the sake
of grief? I couldn't. I wouldn't. And then I realized I didn't even
have the heart to kill. I couldn't euthanize an animal. A life.
It scarred me to hold a dying cat. Her owner's tears pooling.

Daisy shakin' but not cryin'. I couldn't bear it.
I would never have let her go home. Not like that.

I hope she died seconds after he pulled onto the road.
For her sake. After some tears and hard nights he'd survive.
But Daisy didn't deserve to rot.

RAGE

I know that feeling.
The one of a woman's rage.
A solid mass of flame and black tar—
I'd tremble to be on the opposing side.

I first felt it as young as seven when a man
called me "his sunshine". My mom recoiled.
He was a co-worker of hers I never saw again.

I felt it when I was a pre-teen being ogled
at the beach in my tankini. My parents tried
their best to keep me as safe as possible.
A girl is never safe. A woman is never safe.

I was a child (teenagers are children) and I knew
how to look out for predators when my mom dropped
my friend and I off at the mall. We were by ourselves
for the first time ever. I was excited, but cautious.

I knew there was a possibility of being followed,
yet I was still shocked when we were.
My friend caught a white middle-aged man
eying us from across the aisle. She had seen him
in two stores prior doing the same exact thing.
Fucking creep.

We quickly left and dodged him. Mom picked us
up shortly after.

I remember wanting to claw his face off. We had been
so happy and he ruined the entire day.

When I was sixteen, I got a job at Publix as a bagger.
Every single shift I was harassed in some sort of manner
by coworkers, customers, passers-by, etc. I was hugged
from behind without my consent by a male coworker
7 years older than me. Ew.

I wanted to break his legs with a baseball bat.
The guy with the twins who play soccer—
I fantasized about burning him in various ways.
Stabbing is a pretty common method of choice, too.

I've had men grab and caress my arms,
yell and scream profanities and details
of what they would do to me, men cornering
me in a tight space and get little *too* close,
men luring me into the farthest space
in the parking lot with little to no light.

So, yes, I know that feeling.

TWO MONTHS AFTER I STOPPED TAKING BIRTH CONTROL,

the funniest thing happened—
I learned how to feel again.

So many emotions I had forgotten:
how sadness breaks the heart, tears
like a warm kiss on the cheek; you heal
with a feeling of a sweater and hot cocoa.

Or how excitement feels like a fevered
drum going *bang bang thrum* in your chest
and oh boy you better start breathing heavy
because the time has come to run—
like hell is coming up behind you.

I love the days where the sprint
feels like a jolt to my soul.

Happiness is shared in the laughter
of my friends. I'm giddy every time we sit
in front of the television because I know:
I'm in for the best entertainment ever.

I'm learning to love my anger, too. I used to shy
away from it, lock the feeling in a fantasy and call
it a terrible story. But my anger is real and so is my trauma.
I deserve to be angry about everything.

I'm feeling and being kinder to myself.
I never would have thought,
after only two months . . .

I used to be a shadow of a person and now I feel
so much I'm terrified and amazed.
I'm a person again and I am content to know I'm alive.

I'M A HORRIBLE BAKER

I had a few overripe bananas—
Boom! I'll make banana bread I thought.
Easy fix, I found a simple recipe and get moving
with the ingredients. I began pouring this and that
into a bowl. I grabbed the salt—

nearly half a cup pours out. I'm flabbergasted.
Appalled. I can't believe it as I scoop as much
salt as possible out of the bowl—and there still
remains heaps of the damn stuff.

I put my creation in the oven anyways. I had
already bragged to one of my roommates
that I was actually going to bake something edible.
Something she could eat.

I remember watching her try a slice, knowing it would
be salty as hell because my slice was salty as hell.
But she ate her piece with humbleness. She was kind in her
judgement, mentioning the saltiness and crying out
in pity when she heard my story.

She still ate two more slices in the following days,
always when I was in the room.
It was sweet. But god I know she was thirsty.

BARKING

I don't even know why I'm barking.
Is it just because I like being angry?
Do I really wanna stress my heart?
I'm tearing years of life away,
but can I convince myself to care?

I'm looking through a gray fog. I see
hydrangeas, tulips, and crate myrtles,
beautiful colors yet I feel nothing.
I can't touch nature anymore.
The leaves touch my hands, and I hear
no whisper.

I can't hold onto memory very well these
days. I know it's taxing on my friends,
always having to remember for me, answer
all my repeating questions.

I don't even know why I'm barking.
Don't I know I'm ruining my voice?
Don't I know I'll tire myself out until
I drown? My friends are gonna have to pull
me out again, again, and again . . .

LONG BRAIDS

I see her in the smoky moonlight. I'm in a bar
tucked in a corner with no streetlight. There's
a drink half gone. I'm already ready to order
another.

I see her. I blink and I still see her. I rub my eyes
until I'm dizzy and I still see her.

I still see her smooth, dark skin, dimples on her cheeks,
a hazel stare breaking me down like I'm nothing
but a rock in her way. But she chose me—
and we caressed one another perfectly because we
loved how to learn how to love one another.

Her hair was in long braids—

A semi-truck hit her from behind on the inter-state.
Her car turned sideways; she lost control of the wheel . . .

I had to identify the body. I can't imagine what the
wreckage looked like.

I see her, so beautiful, in the moonlight.
But it hurts.

It hurts to love her.

EYE CONTACT

Sometimes I don't meet your eyes
cus' I'm scared the colors inside
will make me think of what it would
feel like to fall in love with you.
I remember wiping your cheeks,
you were crying, saying,
"I don't think I'm pretty."
I didn't know how to tell you
I thought everything about you
was beautiful without you coming
to the conclusion that I'd fallen too far.
So I said, "This feeling will pass.
I bet you'll feel pretty again tomorrow."
Thankfully, I was right.
You felt much better the next day.

That was three years ago.
Your husband probably calls you
beautiful every day.

SEE ME RUIN

Praise me, regain the value in intimacy,
eat your own heart and smile so I can see the blood.
Tell me I'm pretty before you stab me in the back,
make it interesting if you're going to be cruel.

Why do I feel the need to compare tragedies?
I don't need to justify my natural response—
how dare you stare into the maw of an animal
and ask for reasonableness?

This is fucking reasonable. This screaming, raving
crazy woman running after your accountability
you refuse to be aware of. I'll make you swallow your sins.
I'll show you the greatest shit show to ever exist:

A hyperempathetic masochist with a strong sense of justice.
I fucking hate it. I hate feeling so much all the time. I hate
how the blood looks at home between teeth and gums
so far from the consciousness trapped inside this body.

So go ahead, show me your apathy, your misunderstanding
of what I am and what I am capable of feeling.
Give me entertainment and I'll give you an animal in a cage.
See me spit, see me roar, see me ruin the vessel
that renders me incapable of feeling anything other than *everything*.

MY NATURE

My nature requests that I relent comfort
and peace for the sake of empathy. Feel
the weight of the world because how else
can I help the voices screaming in my heart?

Don't you understand—I feel this every day,
all the time there is an ache in my soul, reaching
so far inside my heart sometimes I wonder whether
I can still call myself human.

Maybe if I pretend to be a god, I can justify
my suffering for as long as I live. Maybe if I put
more thought into the work than into the hurt
I can find more reasons to live than to die.

I want to stay, I want to give the beauty of my
own existence to others, to show them it's possible
even if their humanity was once stolen from them.
There is more to life than what I once believed

and yet I am cursed with the weight of the world
paired with the inability to touch the off button.
How could I?

How could I when there are so many voices screaming?

I AM A FEARFUL CREATURE

I accidentally, intentionally made myself
a fearful creature. Eyes peaking around every
corner, locking the car immediately after entering,
always knowing the exits, checking behind my shower
curtain more often than not, sticking keys between fingers
while I stare at strangers staring back. My intention is to be
prepared.

Like a dog trained, a prey animal running on instinct—
I was a girl, so I know the feeling of predator's breath
on the neck. Womanhood had granted me unintentional
opportunities to displease creeps—tattoos, piercings, dyed
hair. I don't dress to please men; I no longer look like a child.

The habits remain, years later. I'm not afraid anymore, but
something in the air doesn't feel right when I don't check,
when I don't get the second glance—

SMILING AT A STRANGER

Can you tell how I'm struggling based on the pages
before? Did you skim through the pages to find this one,
maybe a word or a strange mark on the smooth paper
hooked your interest. Doesn't matter, I guess. Or maybe
it does. Maybe everything matters. Or maybe it doesn't.

I don't think you're reading this, but if you are, I'm happier
now. Believe it or not. Do you remember when we went to
Ripley's Believe It or Not? Everything was so fascinating,
from the ship carved out of jade to the shiny cars behind velvet
rope. Right as we were leaving, we saw a man who was obviously

homeless crouching by the dumpster. We pretended
we didn't see him, walked on.
I didn't feel guilty in that moment.
I do now.

We should have smiled and waved. Acknowledged him
with kindness, somehow. Because why not?
I do a lot of things these days because I ask myself, "Why not?"
We grew up with colorful, thick-lettered signs saying,
"Be the good you want to see in the world."

Do you think I could convince you, despite how I may have
changed, that I have done everything to become the good?
All those pictures of us—the smiling, posed teenagers
waiting for the camera to click. I know I may have looked
happy, and in many ways I was, but god was I so empty.

Empty like I had been carved hollow from the inside out
because I knew so little of what it meant to love unconditionally,
both with myself and with those around me. I hated looking
at my body in the mirror. I didn't like my face. I didn't like my brain
or my hair or my fingers or my personality.

Now I can point to any point on my person and tell you the
    significance,
the beauty. I can find reasons to love even in the darkest of places,
in hateful hearts and fearful bigotry.

I saw you on the other side of a protest yesterday. I don't think
you recognized me. I wondered, "Where's the girl who wrapped arms
around my shoulders, said silly knock knock jokes when I was sad?"
Seconds later, I answered myself—

"She's right where she's chosen to be. Right in front of me, screaming
because I'm protesting against genocide."

I guess we both made our own choices. But I'm not
writing this out of some moral superiority, I'm writing
this because that man crouching by the dumpster outside
of Ripley's Believe It or Not could've been me.
Could've been you, too.

I'd like to believe that if we had a real, thorough, and understanding conversation of what we believed in, we'd reach many similarities.

Maybe it's a good thing, you not recognizing me.

Maybe it can be a good thing because I believe it to be.

Do you think you're a good person just because you believe you are?

Or do strangers feel the love and compassion you have for life and humanity?

Did you feel the love that never faded despite everything when I smiled at you?